The LP Collection:

Lessons and Praise

The LP Collection:

Lessons and Praise

Felecia Karen Scott

To order additional copies of this book, contact:
Xlibris Corporation
0-800-644-6988
www.xlibrispublishing.co.uk
Orders@xlibrispublishing.co.uk
305292

Dedication and Thank You

Before dedicating this book to anyone I would like to honor God for giving me this gift. So I dedicate this book first to Him because He truly is unconditional love. Second, this book is dedicated to my family, friends, and foes you all have truly been inspiration for many of my poems and I am thankful that I am able to share them finally with the world. And most importantly, I am thankful for the patience of the Xlibris staff as they assisted me with this artist journey.

Contents

Return

Eventually everyone is going to return to me
For I am the beginning and the ending and without nothing is possible
All things are possible with me
For I am the Lord and I am so glad my children are returning to me

Who Can? He Can!

Who can weather a storm
Who can make everything all right
Who can answer prayer
Who can take away the pain

He can The Lord can do anything and everything

For He's magnificent
He is excellent
He is a miracle worker

There is not anybody

There is not anybody like the Lord
He will rock you all night long and you will feel secure in his arms
He will give you the strength to journey on
He will make your life so sweet
There is not anybody like Lord
He will protect you through the storm
There is not anybody like the Lord

The Lord's Will

*It is hard to accept what the Lord allows especially when we wanted this to be
the other way*
*But we must understand that He knows best and we are the clay and He is
the potter*
Therefore He molds us and makes us into what we ought to be
And that sometimes includes going to home to glory
Because we got to know how to live heaven on earth
So we can experience a peaceful departure because everything has season
But He knows exactly how we feel
So it is okay to cry
For blessed is ye who mourns and ye shall be comforted
He wants us to cry out to Him
So He can wipe the tears from our eyes
He wants to comfort us and let us know that He is right by our sides
Just know that death is an opening door

There is a healer in the land

He is the only one who can take away the pain which you suffer from head
to toe
For the Lord is the only one who knows the desires of your heart
If you desire healing then He will heal you
For there is a healer in the land and He is the only one who can take away
the pain
There is a healer in the land
He is the only one who can take away all of your pain
He can heal you even if you have the faith of a mustard seed
All you have to do is believe that you are healed
If God said it then He will do it
The Lord is not one to lie
So do not you worry or cry for there is a healer in the land

Doesn't Compare

What you are going through does not compare to what Jesus went through
Jesus was without blemish and you know what they did to Him
So your storm does not compare
Just take it to the Lord in prayer
What you are going through does not compare to what Jesus went through
Jesus was without blemish and you know what they did to Him
What you are going through does not compare to what Jesus went through
Jesus went through
Jesus went through
Jesus went through the storm and the rain so we would not have to experience
the same pain
What you are going through does not compare to what Jesus went through

My love never changes

You will find that a man or a woman will fall in and out of love with you
My love never changes it is always the same just call on my name
I will let you know that my love never changes
My love never changes
Never changes
My love
Never
Changes

The Vessel

YOU could have used another vessel to bring me to the earth but I just want to thank YOU for using the one that you did
The vessel is strong proud wise caring and God fearing
YOU must have known that she is what I need
I also would like to thank YOU for giving her the strength to rear me and giving her so much wisdom
The vessel is no other than my mother
Lord I thank YOU for her
This is indeed a wonderful vessel

He calmed the storm

This particular storm was unlike any other storm
Everyone told her that she would not make it through the storm
After she made it through the storm the same folk that said that she would not
make it through the storm
The same folk asked her How did she make it through
Mother replied that He calmed the storm
They asked her Who is He She told them again the Lord
She said it for last time with a smile He calmed the storm

Satan's Blueprint for the saints

I will entice them with all the riches of the land and make them not focus on God
Although God said in His word that I will supply all of your need according
to my riches in glory by Christ Jesus Phillipians 4:19
I will make unsaved women have the same attributes as same women to keep
men focused on the works of the flesh and not God
I will take the things of their past and put them in their faces
I will convince them that they are not worthy of God because they sin against Him
I will destroy households with lies murder and all types of chaos
I will make them talk about one another and not pay attention in church
I will convince them that the things of the world are better than the things
that the Lord will bless them with by faith
I will cause them to loose their faith in God by confusing them with religion
For these are all of His blueprints therefore make a copy of this blueprint

Felecia Karen Scott

Daughter

Daughter I hear you every time you cry
I know what you are going through and you will smile after awhile
The trial that you are facing is only to make you strong
I bragged about you long ago and I am just completing My job
I am shaping and molding you for your next position
In this position you will face more trials that are why I am allowing you to go through this trial
I know that it seems as if it will never end just have patience
Daughter you are going to win
You just remember to put on your armor
I will hold your hand every step just have faith
Daughter just remember that I have not failed you yet
Even though you may want to throw in the towel
You have to be strong because it is too late for you to turn back now
Daughter I hear you every time you cry
Daughter do not you know that he (Satan) has to ask Me to do whatever he wants to do to you
I signed the permission slip because I bragged about you and I know that you are going to win because you are My child
Daughter you have to cry anymore because your battle is won
Daughter welcome to your new position

Love

There is no love like the Lord's
He loved us before we loved ourselves
No one in the world would do the things that Jesus does for us and no one will
Love
Love allowed him to suffer for us
Love allowed him to save us
Love allowed him to leave us instructions
Love allowed him to protect us
Love
Jesus is the perfect example of love
Love

May you rest in peace in heaven
Where the streets and paved in gold and you will never grow old
*May you rest in peace for you life was not in vain may you rest where you can
not feel any pain*
May you rest in peace where your soul is at total rest
May you rest in heaven where there is nothing but love and happiness
May you rest in peace

Do you see the signs?

Do you see the signs
Is your mind made up
For we are not sure when Lord will return
Do you want to go to heaven
Do you want to see the Lord
Well time is running out

Tomorrow may be too late to get right with God
So Why not do it know
For He is on His way and we do not know how and when He will return
I know that He just want is we to be ready and I want you to know that
Time is running out

Felecia Karen Scott

My Sister

If I had to choose who would be my sister I would always choose you
I have never met someone as meek and true as you
You always come to my rescue in when I needed you
If you have any pain if I had to for you I would bleed
If I had to compare you with any of my friends you would always be number one
I can always count on you for strength guidance and comfort
I have always admired your strength intelligence and wisdom
In other words I want to you how much I love you

Who are we?

We are human beings made of flesh blood and spirit
We are God's creation for we possess beauty wisdom and intelligence
We are strong noble kind creative humble proud angry soulful caring
mysterious misunderstood and God-fearing but what is most important is that
we are the blueprints for all mankind
So if you were unsure of our identity then ask yourself again Who are we
For I have explained who we are therefore the mystery has been solved
The next time you ask the question who are we The answer would be God's
perfect creation

FELECIA KAREN SCOTT

Thanks in advance

You pay your bills early so you do not have to worry about the collectors In fact
you give them a little extra in advance just to thank them for their services

So why not do the Lord the same way
Just Thank Him in advance

Lord we just want to say Thanks in advance
Thanks in advance for the blessings that You are going to bestow upon the earth
Thanks in advance for the souls that you saved

God versus Satan

He destroys (Satan)
But
He rebuilds (God)
But
He deceives (Satan)
But
He loves (God)
But
He hates (Satan)
But
He sacrifices (God)
But
He use many unorthodox devices (Satan)
But
He heals (God)
But
He inflicts pain (Satan)
But
He is everlasting (God)
While
He is temporary (Satan)

FELECIA KAREN SCOTT

The Prayer Closet

You can go a place when they feel that all hope is gone
You feel like there is no one around that understands you and the thing that
you are going through it is the prayer closet
Do not feel like God's is not going to take care of you because you have
disappointed Him for He is the same today tomorrow and yesterday
So all you have to do is pray and if you can't pray for yourself go to someone
who can get a prayer through but you just go to the prayer closet
Go to the prayer closet in that closet you find peace joy relief comfort a healer
a counselor a lover and a friend
The prayer closet is always open
So go

Seek His face

The Lord desires for us to seek His face instead of arguing about which religion is right or wrong For He left us the Bible to read for instruction and not destruction but He would like for us to lead not unto our own understanding but to be patient and He will reveal Himself to us Not all He asks is for us to seek His face we because He has suffered for us so would not be lost

Don't be discouraged

I know sometimes our family and friends mistreat us and it hurts us but do not be discouraged for that is not your battle You have to pray for them and be patient because we glory in tribulations also: knowing that tribulation works patience: and patience experience: and experience hope Romans 5:3-4
Do not be discouraged for everything is going to be all right
For weeping may endure for a night but joy comes in the morning
So do not be discouraged for that is not your battle Don't you know that trial come to make you strong so don't you worry and just praise the Lord for your circumstance in the meanwhile and after you do you will wear a smile

Never Alone

*Sometimes you feel a little lonely but the Lord wants you to know that you
are never alone not as long as I am around just don't take you hand out of
my hand*
*When you feel like you cannot call on anyone I want you know that I am
always here for you For my love for you will never change and I am never too
busy too listen to your cry and I will run to your side Son you are never alone
I will replace the things and loved ones which you have lost I will make you
whole again for I am your Father as well as your friend There is not any heart
that I cannot mend just lean on me for I just want you to know that you are
never alone Daughter you have been searching for love in all of the wrong
places and you know that I love you so don't feel compelled to be with someone
just because your peers are in what they think is love*

Inspiration

The Lord and His word
My mother her wisdom and love
My father and his love for wisdom
My sister her strength
My grandmother her life her love and her words
My family
My friends
My foes
My life
Encouragement from others
Others lives
Heartbreaks and disappointments

Mother planted the seed

I can recall when I was down
My mother told me to write my feelings down
As I began to write my words began to speak to me
Little did I know she was planting the seed and this seed became some of my
best poetry
For mother planted the seed

FELECIA KAREN SCOTT

The Sacrificial Lamb

It was April when the Lord called you home
Your mother signed a petition with God for you because she knew that you
wanted to see her one more time
Your mother had a dream for all of her children to continue to seek the Lord
You and your sisters and brothers accepted Him as children
Her dream was for all of children to be saved
Therefore you were called home
As a result of you being called home it brought the family together and many
of the family members were saved and began to attend church because they
want to see you again
You were indeed the sacrificial lamb

Using

You will never know whom the Lord is using
No you will never know
He can use the sinner as well as the saint because He knows that He will be
glorified
He was the same one who used Moses despite of his case
He used Moses because He is the Great I am
So you never know who the Lord is using

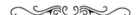

Food

In search for nourishment we often settle for the food which is given to us
It is not until we find out that food which is given to us is detrimental to our health
It is detrimental to our health because it often creates diseases that can only be cured by the Creator
The food which I am referring to are the words that individuals have used to either help us or destroy us
The nourishment that we receive from this food only makes us crave what we truly deserve
That is food which is disease free that is good to the body and soul
The food that we deserve is the food that keeps our spirits free our hearts and minds clear and our flesh healthy
The food that we deserve is the truth
We have been eating unhealthy food for too long and if we continue to eat it then more disease will be created

Hold on

Hello I want to know can I get a prayer through I have been going through somethings that are beyond my understanding Sometimes I think it Satan trying to attack me and other times I think it the Lord preparing me for my victory Mam Hold on okay

The operator of the pray request line left the woman on hold

The woman called another prayer request line and the operator told her to hold on

She called her best friend and he said hold on

She tried to get everyone to pray for her but everyone told her to hold on

She got tired of holding on and then it dawned on her that she needed to pray for herself and that why God made everyone she called to place on hold

She prayer and waited for God's reply and her told her to hold on

The message is to hold on and it will be better after awhile

FELECIA KAREN SCOTT

Lady

Mama said to be a lady at all times although people say and do things to blow your mind
She said baby you got to lay low and possess a gentle demeanor
She said that is the main ingredient of being a lady
She said that you can not let your anger get the best of you cause you know the trick of the enemy
Mama said to be a lady and a lady uses discretion
Discretion is powerful
She also said that the best words are the ones that are not said

Baby Lay Low
You know how the wind blows
Sometimes it is best that folk don't know what you know
Sometimes you want to explode but be a lady all times
You may want curse but that isn't right she says because it just opens up another can of worms
Be a Lady
Be a Lady
Be a lady even when you feel like it isn't necessary
You kill more bees with honey

Daddy says remember that you are a queen
So baby wear your crown proudly
Daddy said that there is nothing more attractive than an intelligent and independent lady

Mama and Daddy say to be a lady
So take heed but what is most important is that you are yourself
So sisters please be ladies

I'm that Sister

I am that sister who you disrespected in the past
I am that same sister who you needed then and still need now
I am that sister who knew all of life's games
I am that sister who when you need something you would call my name
I am that sister whom in the past you were ashamed of but I am that same
sister who continues to love you
I am that sister who kindness you took for weakness and I am that same sister
who knows the key to your happiness
For I am that sister The sister in the time of adversity

Who is Your Friend?

Everybody needs somebody in his or her time of need
Who can you call on Who will help you weather the storm
Who is your friend Will this friend stick closer than a brother will
Will this friend treat you like no other Will this friend be there for you
Will this person love you for you So Who is your friend

Who can you call on No not one
Who will help you weather the storm Only the Lord
Who is your friend Nobody but the Lord
Will this friend stick closer than a brother will Yes
Will this friend treat you like no other will Yes
Will this friend be there for you Yes
Will this friend love you for you Yes
So Who is your friend I hope and pray that your friend is the Lord
For you will always find peace in his arms
His love is real and He is real for I know He is friend who you ought to know
So I am asking you again who is your friend

Instruction

No one knows exactly when the Lord will return
He just wants us to be prepared so He left an instruction manual for us
He left it for us to follow but in it he said that it is our decision
In His manual He also put in it what would happen to us if we did not
follow it
Follow the instruction manual and you will be prepared when the Lord returns

Investments

You have read through all the pamphlets
Reading line for line
You even read the fine print
You read the fine print that is in the fine print
Yet your are constantly going over the material
So you will not miss anything
However you have read and reviewed until you find yourself reading and
reviewing over and over again
Since you are hesitant about signing the dotted line you are reluctant
Previously you lost stock but was left with bonds that you can only use
Wisely and not return
So these are the premises for you not making any bad investments

No Pun Intended

Sometimes you have every right to retaliate
Something inside summons you to hold your peace at the moment
So you can diplomatically handle the matter
After diplomatically handling the matter you feel the need to vent
Venting to those that understand and confirm that vengeance is the Lord's
In the midst of your venting you say a few obscenities to illustrate your current anger
That is when wisdom reveals what becomes of the brokenhearted
You choose to take heed because right now you do not need an untimely demise
Because you don't want to ruin your reputation for handling things with stride
There is always pride before a fall
So you choose to stand tall
Realistically after it is all said and done there was truly no pun intended

Daily Greeting

Each day He greets me with new mercies
Often by another level excellence
Providing me ideas that are targeted towards my success
My success is not measured by man
But by the things which He has placed in me
Like the ability to convey my ideas through words melody and movement
Because He has given me this divine groove
A groove that has the ability to communicate spirit and flesh
Often this groove needs no music
Since the melody is hidden behind the flow of rhythm
Relishing in the thought that He thought so highly of me that He granted me
another day to perfect the work that He started in me
So I thank Him for this daily greeting
This greeting feeds me better than my mom's beefaroni
Although she cooks everything with love

Deep yet shallow

Unfortunately you are knee deep into an abyss of chaos
This chaos has you thinking that the truths are lies and that lies are truth
For wearing masks is your full time masquerade
You claim you keep it real but your reality is a fabricated image an image you developed for acceptance
How can you expect folk to accept you when it is clear that you battle with self hate
So you self medicate
The depth of your intelligence is measured by those who you assume are beneath you or appear to be on the same level
You thrive off of giving constructive criticism when in fact you are being overly critical and you have the audacity to tell folk not to judge
Being aware of ways that need to be changed but you rebel in the name of being yourself
So self preservation is your mantra
Yet selfishness is unforeseen since generosity is the glue that connect you to people
These same people see you wading in a shallow pool
A shallow pool because your observations and conclusions regarding others is so unreal but you real deep
Deep like the water that drowned you with sorrow
Sorrow simply because you did recognize your own beauty

FELECIA KAREN SCOTT

Let me

Let me hold your hand when times are hard
Let me let you know that it is okay to let down your guard
Let me help you to seize the day
Let me be the one that wipes your invisible tears
Let me see you through how God see you
Let me awaken the sweet spirit that lies in you
Just let me

Samples keep you thirsty

Insatiable appetite
Willing to accommodate compromise confront and possibly avoid anything that infers with pleasure
Pleasure that takes on a fragrance that solidifies moments that can't be reactivated yet a sample only makes you want more when you know less is given due to selfishness

This poems was inspired by Dr. Ty Adams book Single, Saved and Having Sex it is definitely a must read along with my spiritual father and pastor Pastor James Polly sermons about how you know the truth and like a dog return to your vomit.

FELECIA KAREN SCOTT

My Brother

In law does not define how you feel about me
And vice versa yet you know me
You know how to correct protect and advise in a way that I answer my own
concerns
Your sarcasm invisible tears honesty and love okay let's not get too mushy
Perhaps you are even wondering why I am getting my poetry published
But then again whatever makes me happy right as long as is in reason
Always wanted a brother
But wasn't sure if I wanted you after all I have my sister with you
Yet I have gained so much from you being in my life and I refuse to let you be
too long out of my sight
Just want you know brother like you there is no other

Hey Beautiful

From afro's to weaves
Sister's we are queens
Embracing our dreams with a boldness that utters that we are children of the Most High
Destined for greatness so we have to keep our eyes on the prize
Recognizing that we are what God says that we are
And if He says that we are great then that is what we are
Sometimes you got to walk out of something in order to walk into something better than you imagined
Because grace and mercy to us is granted but cannot be abused
And through the blood sweat and tears sometimes you have to at the end of the day look at yourself and say Hey beautiful

FELECIA KAREN SCOTT

Unknown Soldiers

Tomb of the unknown soldiers
These soldiers are unknown
But their spirits run freely for they still create art on the walls
These spirits constantly erase and re-write hieroglyphics on these walls creating
similar drawings each time yet there is no rest for these spirits in the tomb of
unknown soldiers
Because although the soldiers are unknown their spirits are well know due to
the art wihich on the walls

Got to

Got to hold my peace today
Because I am on trial
I do not want to prosecute myself today
Has been predestined go to learn this important lesson
It's purpose is to take me to another level
Go to be quick to listen and not respond
If I do then I have fallen into the trap

FELECIA KAREN SCOTT

Wandering Eye

I am your sweet thing
But your appetite for real love
Got your eye wandering
Cause you never knew a love like this before
Cause a love like this requires more patience and understanding
After all you never imagined meeting your own reflection with a few minor
imperfections that remind you of your former self
So we fight due to the lack of understanding
But that does not stop the fact that for now you have a wandering eye
Although you are convinced that you are too busy and not focused
Your justification for your action but did you know that few words are
profound and some explanations are simply unnecessary
Cause brother it is obvious that you have a wandering eye

Mother's Wisdom

Mother's Wisdom
Is equated
With Being
Old School
But her school
Is not old
Just that
Being Virtuous
Is most important
To her and ensuring that
Her seeds
Follow the same values
Although she is aware of mistakes
Mother's Wisdom Is
Often Envied
She Keeps Things Tight
When Everyone's
World Seems to be
Going in circles
Unfortunately she cries differently
For she cries out to God first and not man for she knows that He has never
Failed her yet because He calmed the storm and is the Light of the world
That is why mother's wisdom is not old school

My Sunshine

My sunshine in the rain embraces me with gentle heat
That reminds me of a comforter or an electric blanket
Providing an energy that eases pain and feels quite cozy
But this energy lasts after the rain
Still producing sunshine and rainbows

Crying   *All*
Soothes   *Tears*
Pain   *For*
But   *The*
There   *Lord*
Is   *Is*
Not   *Near*
Enough   *To*
Tissue   *Near*
To   *Too*
Wipe   *Provide*
Tears   *Comfort*
But
Prayer
Heals
All
Things
And
Dries
All
Tears
For

Invisible Tears

Tears are invisible yet they are seen for they are only traces of a clown
So I enjoy pretending that everything is okay when I often don't want to exist
If I could sleep my pain away
If I could sleep my pain away
But I got to live because my purpose has not been fulfilled
Tears are invisible yet they are seen for they are only traces of a clown
So I enjoy pretending that everything is okay when I often don't want to exist

Temptation's Smile

Temptation's smile is masked with war paint
For this war is unseen but seen due to the elements
Which are currently in the universe

Blinded

You are blinded by darkness and unfortunately your eyes are too green to see the light
The light that beams through all of my imperfection because my imperfections are my perfections because they keep me on my knees or better yet constantly talking to God
So He can allow you to see my true beauty
I mean my intellect and not only my competence
The point is you misjudge your own
Therefore you do not trust my competence
You will remind everyone of my mistakes but anyway let us not discuss that because God knows the facts
So as long as He has me then your opinions are irrelevant
However you are still blinded by darkness

No Friend like Him

Consistent when I am inconsistent
Comforts when I need comforting
Listens to my heart
Grants me new mercies
Gives me peace when storms are raging
Let's me by myself while shaping and molding me
Directs and corrects
Serenades me with sunshine kisses
Picks me up and places me on His back so I can only see His footprints
He wants me to only see His footprints so my steps can continue to be ordered Him
Made the ultimate sacrifice because He loves me just that much
So just wanted to let you know that there is No Friend like Him

Year Overview

Kept blessing me
Blessing with understanding
Understanding to match my knowledge
Wisdom to practically apply faith
Knowing that with Him I am nothing but with Him I am more than my
imagination
Certain that I am His child so mediocrity is not tolerated
As our relationship grows deeper I have no choice than to reach the level of
excellence which for He created for me
So if I am awakened by Him I must write the vision and make it plain and
in the process ask and wait for instruction
But all year long He kept blessing me

Queen Destiny

Calls like freedom
And responds
Like wisdom
For her majesty
Adorns her in purple
For she is royalty
Her spirit sparkles like a diamond
For she is a precious jewel
A precious jewel for she was created in the likeness of the Creator
And trust He makes no mistakes
Yet some find her essence breathtaking
While others use her influence for selfish reasons
Yet Queen Destiny
Reigns over all heartbreaks and disappointments
See she refuses to see any dream deferred
Because she obeys the commands of the Most High God
So ladies it is time to ignite the power
The power that was placed in you for the true essence of a Queen is in you so go and claim your destiny

Definition of Switching

Lips saying you get none
Hips saying come and get some
And you are wondering why the brother's on the basketball court and giving
you inordinate affection
All because you don't know the definition of switching

This Love

This love was aware of me prior to conception
For I was formed in the conception of His imagination
His imagination led Him to placing in the ability to use my limbs to
communicate the language between flesh and spirit
I was created to keep a unique harmony and rhythm that is for Him and
only Him
So with my limbs I thank Him cause this love
This love keeps me grounded
This love allows me to release toxins my mind and my body
It uplifts viewers while also provoking a level of scrutiny
This love frees me from all calamities
For this love is praise
Praise without and with cymbals
Praise with a mighty hand clap
Praise with a sweet song in the midnight hour
Praise with a leap
Praise with a dance
This love

FELECIA KAREN SCOTT

Life's Negoitables

Assets versus liabilities
Principle versus interest
Priorities versus options
Plus versus minus
Rich versus poor
Love versus hate
Needs versus wants
Life versus death
Choose to be an asset
Balance principle and interest
Understand your priorities while weighing your options
Recognize your plusses and reflect on your minus
Strive to live richly while empowering the poor
Love humanity and eradicate hate
Make your needs a priorities and wants the vehicle that foster's your dream
Live life to the fullest why understanding that death should be the final destination

Children

Breath of innocence
Ready to explore
What the world offers
Fearing what is seen and trusting what is not
Absorbing the essence of the world's fruit and labor
Giving clarity to learning by reminding and reciprocating all that have been learning by watching or listening or listening while watching always sleeping peacefully with one eye open and the other shut
While the eye that is shut is communicating with the third and the third eye and the third eye is no other than Jesus
Adapting to challenges without adapting still ready and able to conquer and explore the world with a sober heart and a open mind and a closed mouth
The same closed mouth that can only penetrate or produce fruitful words that are eloquent although the vocabulary is not fine tuned referred to as lambs yet humans with simplicity and honesty
Welcome to the brief description and definition our children

FELECIA KAREN SCOTT

So many names and so many faces

So many names and so many faces just because people want to physically identify with the Almighty
The Almighty told Moses that I am the great I am
Geography and history sets the tone
Created the institution called religion
This same institution cause division amongst the body of believers
Man made doctrines and philosophies has created a circle of decievers
Separating church and state for their own sakes
Wearing masks and dictating behavior in the name of their savior
All because people want to physically identify with the Almighty
It is spiritual and not physical folk simply do not understand
So many names
So many faces
All because people want to physically identify with the Almighty
Looking for that perfect leader who always marches to the beat the most perfect drummer
Can not see that the only perfect drummer was still is Jesus
Yet God has so many names and so many faces just because people want to identify physically with the Almighty
Looking at vessel instead of the perfect examples left in all of His famous storybooks
Fighting over who is and who is wrong instead of agreeing to agree to disagree
Establishing a personal relationship with Almighty is the only way to identify with Him physically
Yet He still has so many manes and so many faces

This poem inspired by a conversation with my parents regarding how the three major religions under Mosaic Law are so similar yet our intellect breeds confusion and false hope. Glad that daddy had a chance to hear and see this poem before going home to glory.

Edwards Brothers Malloy
Thorofare, NJ USA
September 9, 2014